Bannockburn School Dist. 106
2165 Telegraph Road
Bannockburn, Illinois 60015

DATE DUE

FOLLETT

Bannockburn School Dist. 106
2165 Telegraph Road
Bannockburn, Illinois 60015

Musical Families

The Brass Family on Parade!

by Trisha Speed Shaskan

illustrated by Robert Meganck

PICTURE WINDOW BOOKS
a capstone imprint

Special thanks to our advisers for their expertise:

Rick Orpen, PhD, Professor of Music, Gustavus Adolphus College
Terry Flaherty, PhD, Professor of English, Minnesota State University, Mankato

Picture Window Books
151 Good Counsel Drive
P.O. Box 669
Mankato, MN 56002-0669
877-845-8392
www.capstonepub.com

Editor: Jill Kalz
Designer: Lori Bye
Art Director: Nathan Gassman
Production Specialist: Jane Klenk
The illustrations in this book were
created digitally.

Printed in the United States of America in North Mankato, Minnesota
032010
005740CGF10

 All books published by Picture Window Books
are manufactured with paper containing at least
10 percent post-consumer waste.

Library of Congress Cataloging-in-Publication Data
Shaskan, Trisha Speed, 1973–
The brass family on parade! / by Trisha Speed Shaskan ;
illustrated by Robert Meganck.
p. cm. – (Musical families)
Includes index.
ISBN 978-1-4048-6041-4 (library binding)
1. Brass instruments–Juvenile literature. I. Meganck, Robert. II. Title.
ML933.S496 2011
788.9'19–dc22   2010001087

Bonjour! My name is Fifi, and I'm a French horn. My husband, Max, is a tuba. Our son Tiny is a trumpet, and our son Slim is a trombone. Together, we're the Brass family.

MAX, the tuba

TINY, the trumpet

SLIM, the trombone

We're called brass instruments because our bodies are usually made of brass.

mouthpiece

We each have a mouthpiece at one end of our bodies.

We have a bell at the other end.

bell

In between is a tube. When air flows through the tube, we make sound.

Brass instruments are played around the world. But they're not always made of metal. They can be made of bamboo, animal horns, or even seashells.

Even though we belong to the same family,
we all make different sounds.

Max **burps** out loud,
low notes.

I have a
soft sound.

6

Tiny **screams.**

He can hit the highest notes.

Slim's sound slides all over the place.

7

It can get noisy around our house!

Sometimes I have to tell the kids to put a mute in their bells.

 A mute changes an instrument's sound, usually by softening it. Mutes come in different sizes and styles. They can be used with any brass instrument.

Each member of my family has a different shape. But people play us the same basic way.

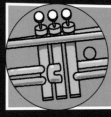

Valves control the air moving through a brass instrument. They can be pressed one at a time or in combination (groups) to change notes.

To play a brass instrument, musicians buzz their lips against the mouthpiece.

Buzzzzz!

Then they blow into the tube.

Wooooosh!

Musicians can make different sounds by placing their lips on the mouthpiece in different ways.

Take a look at Max. He's a big instrument, isn't he? A musician needs a lot of air to play a tuba.

Breathe!
Blow!
Breathe!
Blow!

Now look at Slim. He doesn't have valves like the rest of us. He has a slide. To play a trombone, a musician should have long arms. He needs to move the slide back and forth to play different notes.

The French horn is the hardest brass instrument to play.

I can be stubborn!

A musician pushes the valves with her left hand. She cups her right hand and places it inside the bell. It's important for air to flow through the instrument in just the right way.

Despite its name, most forms of the French horn were invented in Germany. Today, many people just call it the horn.

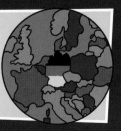

Tiny the trumpet is the smallest and most common brass instrument. But he has a big, special place in our family.

Trumpets announce things!

Today, for example, Tiny stood on the balcony and squealed. I knew something exciting was about to begin.

The Greeks thought the trumpet sounded like an elephant. Today, people still say elephants "trumpet."

Max was dancing on the street below. He puffed out some long, deep notes. Before I could say,

"Ooh-la-la!"

Tiny ran outside to join him.

Slim and I started playing too. We love jazz music!
Slim used his hand and a mute to make a
WAH-WAH sound.

African-Americans were the first
people to play jazz. It was born
in the southern United States
about 100 years ago. Jazz
musicians often improvise, or
add their own notes to the music.

Before long, the whole neighborhood was making music.

20

The Percussion family marched over. There was Sticks the snare drum and Barry the bass drum. Sticks tap-tapped. Barry boom-boomed. They added rhythm.

Then Clara the clarinet and Slick the saxophone joined in. They're part of the Woodwind family down the street.

Rhythm is the flow of sound in music that has regular beats.

People all over town heard the sound and gathered on the street.

They clapped.   They sang.   They danced.   And we played all day long.

Glossary

bell—the flared end of a wind instrument; sound comes out of the bell

brass—a type of yellow metal

mouthpiece—the part of a wind instrument into which a musician blows

musician—a person who plays music

mute—a tool used to change a musical instrument's sound

rhythm—a pattern of beats

valve—a device that controls the flow of air through an instrument

Fun Facts

To play a French horn, a musician puts her right hand inside the instrument's bell. This move is called hand stopping. A musician changes the pitch (how high or low a note sounds) by moving her hand inside the bell.

Louis Armstrong was one of the best jazz trumpet players in history. He also sang. He began his music career in New Orleans, Louisiana. In the 1920s, he was paid 15 cents a night to play music.

A trombone slide is made of a small tube that fits into a bigger tube. To play lower notes, a musician pulls the slide out. To play higher notes, she pushes the slide in.

Brass instruments can play in an orchestra. An orchestra is a group of musicians who play together on various instruments, especially violins and other string instruments.

23

To Learn More

More Books to Read

Knight, M.J. *Brass and Woodwinds.* Musical Instruments of the World. North Mankato, Minn.: Smart Apple Media, 2006.

Koscielniak, Bruce. *The Story of the Incredible Orchestra.* Boston: Houghton Mifflin Co., 2000.

McDonough, Yona Zeldis. *Who Was Louis Armstrong?* New York: Grosset & Dunlap, 2004.

Internet Sites

FactHound offers a safe, fun way to find Internet sites related to this book.

All of the sites on FactHound have been researched by our staff.

Here's all you do:

Visit *www.facthound.com*

FactHound will fetch the best sites for you!

Index

Look for all the books in the Musical Families series:

Around the World with the Percussion Family!

The Brass Family on Parade!

The Keyboard Family Takes Center Stage!

Opening Night with the Woodwind Family!

The String Family in Harmony!